How to read Bible references:

Matthew 24:35 = The Gospel according to Matthew, chapter 24, verse 35

CW01582404

Word of Hope Ministries

ISBN: 978-1-908392-01-5

Why weren't we born in heaven (paradise)?

E. M. Hicham

Serious Answers to Sincere Questions

Have you ever thought about the following two questions? Why weren't we born in heaven (paradise)? Why is there death?

These are very important questions. To find the answers, we must go back to the beginning, to creation. We need to grasp what happened in the Garden of Eden (جنة عدن).

How did it all begin?

Everything about the world that God made was good. There was plenty of food and drink for every living creature. It was in this lovely setting that the first people, Adam and Eve, lived. If they had continued to live for Him, obeying Him, they would have lived *forever;* but God told them that if they disobeyed Him *they would surely die*. God commanded Adam, saying, "Of every tree of the garden you may freely eat; but of the tree of the knowledge of good and evil you shall not eat, for in the day that you eat of it *you shall surely die.*" (Bible, Torah, Genesis 2:16-17) God's warning was clear: disobedience leads to death.

God wanted them to live forever worshipping Him. God gave them a precious gift: free will! He did not make them like robots so that they would *have to* love and obey Him. Love must come freely. This gift of free will was one of the main differences between mankind and the animals. Adam and Eve could choose between right and wrong, good and bad. They could choose to do what God wanted or what they wanted, to live for God or for themselves.

They chose to disobey God! They preferred to please themselves rather than God.

Why did they do this? What went wrong?

It was the devil, Satan (شيطان – a name which means "the deceiver"), who tempted the first man and woman to choose wrong and disobey God. Adam and Eve ignored God's warning. The consequence? Death – spiritual and physical, as God had warned. *"The wages of sin is death,"* as the Bible expresses it. (Bible, Injil, Romans 6:23) Adam and Eve immediately died spiritually when they disobeyed. What did spiritual death mean? It meant that their personal relationship with God was now broken because of their sin. Then, they were expelled from the Garden of Eden, the place where God was present in a special way. The expulsion from the garden illustrates the reality of their relationship with God being broken. It is because Adam died spiritually that he died physically several hundred years later. Adam and Eve would not have died if they had not disobeyed God. We see here the holiness of God and His moral obligation to condemn those who sin against Him. He cannot tolerate one single sin! Nor will He change what He has once declared.

Was Adam's sin just an accident?

No! Was it just ignorance? Was it just forgetfulness? Not at all! It was a deliberate choice to believe Satan's lie. It was disbelieving God and reckoning himself to be perfectly capable of looking after himself and going his own way. And that is the mind-set of every human being born into this world since Adam.

Suppose God said to a gardener, "I want you to trim these bushes by three o'clock this afternoon. But be careful. There is a large open pit at the edge of the garden. If you fall into that pit, you will not be able to get yourself out. So whatever you do, stay away from that pit." Suppose that as soon as God leaves the gardener runs over and jumps into the pit. At three o'clock God returns and finds the bushes untrimmed. He calls for the gardener and hears a faint cry from the edge of the garden. He walks to the edge of the pit and sees him helplessly flailing around on the bottom. He says, "Why haven't you trimmed the bushes as I asked you?" The gardener replies angrily, "How do you expect me to trim the bushes when I am trapped in this pit? If you hadn't left this empty pit here, I wouldn't be in this predicament."

Adam's sin was not an accident or an act of ignorance. Adam didn't simply slip into sin; he jumped deliberately into it with both feet. He jumped into the pit. Adam was clearly warned about it. God had told him to stay away. The consequences Adam experienced from being in the pit were a direct punishment for jumping deliberately into it.

Was Adam's sin forgiven?

I know that Muslims believe that Adam and Eve sinned against God, but that they afterwards repented and that their repentance was accepted

– with the effect that everything came back to normal again, and the divine plan prescribed for Adam and Eve took its due course.

If that was the case, my friend, why were they punished? Why were they left to die? All Muslims accept that Adam and Eve were driven out of the Garden when they sinned. If Adam and Eve were forgiven and things returned to normal, why weren't they allowed back into the Garden? They were never permitted to re-enter, nor has any subsequent member of the human race entered.

Adam - a federal headship!

The Torah (Tawrat) tells us that when God first created the universe, He appointed one man to represent us in the Garden of Eden (جنة عدن). The Hebrew name "Adam" means *mankind*. Adam was God's perfect choice for you and me. Just as a federal government has a chief spokesman, or representative, who is the head of the nation, so Adam was the federal head of mankind. My relationship with God depends on my representative's relationship with God. And so when Adam disobeyed, all mankind disobeyed! Sin (like poison) entered into our world and into human life.

Think of it like a set of dominoes. You can stand them all up in a long line. But if the first one falls down, what will happen to the rest? They will all fall too. In the same way, when the first man fell, all the rest of mankind fell too. Adam's fall was our fall. This is what Christians mean by "the inheritance of original sin". When God punished Adam by causing him to die, we were all likewise punished – we all die too. The curse of the fall affects us all.

The Hadith on the concept of the inheritance of Adam's sin

For Christians the Qur'an and Hadith are not authoritative but, since Muslims draw their beliefs from these two sources, I would like to remind them that the concept of the inheritance of original sin is obviously present in the Hadith in which Adam explicitly bears responsibility for humanity's exile from paradise: "Allah's apostle [Muhammad] said, 'Adam and Moses met, and Moses said to Adam, "*You are the one who made people miserable and turned them out of Paradise.*"'" (Hadith, Bukhari, vol. 6, book 65, no. 4736) This clearly teaches that the human race shares in Adam's exile.

Is it fair?

What have we seen so far? The consequence of Adam's sin was death. Any serious thinker should come to the same conclusion. But if we look at Adam's offspring (including ourselves) we find them suffering the same punishment of death as well. We are therefore faced with one of two conclusions:

- Adam represented his descendants, in which case it is fair and just for his descendants to receive part of the punishment..., or,
- Adam did not represent his descendants, in which case the

infliction of punishment for sin on those who had no part in his fall is a great evil and manifest injustice – and God Himself is unjust!

Let me put it simply. If I have nothing to do with Adam's sin, then why should I share the consequence of his sin? Why wasn't I born in paradise? If I was born perfect (as Muslims believe), then, to be fair, God should have created me in paradise (as He did with Adam) and waited to see if I would disobey like Adam and Eve did. But He didn't, did He? I wasn't born in paradise!

The truth is that, as a result of what happened in the Garden of Eden, each of us is born with an insurmountable gap between us and God. We have all inherited Adam's sin. This is why we were not born in paradise. The prophet David wrote, *"Behold, I was brought forth in iniquity, and in sin my mother conceived me."* (Bible, Psalm 51:5) This is very true! Think about children. One of the first words little children pronounce is "no"! We all know their very early disobedience. Does anyone teach them how to be naughty? Do you think children need to be taught how to disobey? Of course not! Parents teach them good behaviour, but no one needs to teach them naughtiness. By nature they know how to be naughty! It's in them from birth. What the prophet David said is absolutely true – we are born in iniquity, and in sin our mothers conceived us!

God is holy and we are sinful, so we are cut off from Him. A prophet said, *"Your iniquities have separated you from God; and your sins have hidden His face from you."* (Bible, Isaiah 59:2)

To sum it up we could say that you and I are justly due the same punishment as Adam because we are as disobedient and fallen as he was. This is why we were not born in paradise.

What is the solution?

So much for the bad news about man; now for the good news. It is God's solution! People want to have their own solutions, but we should always and only look at the solution that God has provided.

What did God do when Adam and Eve disobeyed? Did He destroy them? He could have done so. Did He say to them, "If you want to return to paradise then you must do more good deeds (حسنات) than bad deeds (سيآت)"? No, no! No amount of good deeds could cancel out their sin.

So what was God's remedy for sin and its consequence, death? We read in the Torah that after Adam and Eve sinned, God gave a promise:

"So the Lord God said to the serpent: 'Because you have done this, you are cursed more than all cattle, and more than every beast of the field; on your belly you shall go, and you shall eat dust all the days of your life. And I will put enmity between you and the woman, and between your seed and her Seed; He shall bruise your head, and you shall bruise His heel.'" (Bible, Torah, Genesis 3:14-15)

Thank God that we find not only His holiness displayed here, but also His mercy. God's words to Satan are called "the first good news". What does God promise here? He promises a redeemer or deliverer

– the seed of the woman (who is called "He"). This is a prophecy of a virgin birth. Notice that He doesn't say the seed of the man and the woman, but the seed of the woman, full stop. In other words, God said, "I am a holy God. I don't tolerate sin. I told you that the consequence of sin is death. I cannot just ignore sin. I must deal with it. There is only one remedy for sin and death. It is through what a Person will one day do. He will save you and crush the power of Satan. This Person will not have a human father. He will come only from a woman."

Now my dear friend, tell me: Who do you know in all of human history who was born only of a woman? Who, in all of human history, never had a human father? Yes, you have the right answer – only Jesus Christ! He was conceived by the Holy Spirit in Mary's womb. He is the fulfilment of God's promise here.

Can we be sure of going to paradise?

"I wish I could be sure!" my friend said, "but there's no way for me to know if I'm going to paradise or hell. I try to live a decent life, but I'll have to wait until the Day of Judgement to see where God will put me... Right now, I don't know where that will be."

"Wouldn't it be nice,' I asked, 'to be sure that if you died you'd go straight to paradise?"

"No one at all can be sure of going to paradise,' he answered, 'Do you know anyone who's sure?"

"Yes, I know someone," I replied, "I am."

'How dare you say that!" he shouted.

And then he left. Perhaps you would have said the same thing! Consider the following story about a wicked man who went to paradise. It is found in the Gospel account, Injil, Luke 23:33-43.

An evil man who went to paradise!

It was nine o'clock in the morning when they nailed Jesus to a cross.[1] Two thieves were crucified at the same time. The Bible tells us that Jesus was in the middle, with one thief on His right and the other on His left. These two thieves were probably members of a violent gang led by a man called Barabbas. If so, they were merciless criminals who cut throats, robbed houses and violated women. They were greedy, cruel and unkind.

From 9am till noon, people walked by the three crosses, throwing insults and mockery into Jesus' face. Both thieves did the same. Yet, by twelve o'clock, Jesus had promised that one of them would go to paradise. Something big must have happened between 9 and 12 that morning!

The thief was suddenly overwhelmed by a sense of God and the guilt of his own sin. He realised that the Person he was insulting (Jesus) was the pure and sinless King. So he prayed to Jesus saying, "Lord, remember me when You come into Your kingdom."

[1] E.M. Hicham has written a booklet called, "Did Jesus really die?" Contact us if you'd like a free copy.

(Bible, Injil, Luke 23:42) Here we see that this thief had faith. Jesus Christ answered him and said, "Assuredly, I say to you, **today** you will be with Me in **Paradise**" (Bible, Injil, Luke 23:43) In Greek the word "assuredly" means IT IS FIXED and IT CANNOT BE CHANGED. Jesus told this man (an evil thief, remember) that he would go to paradise, THAT DAY. And we don't read that Jesus said anything else to him at all. The man didn't need to hear any-thing else did he?

TODAY	: What speed!
WITH ME	: What company!
IN PARADISE	: What happiness!

Just before Jesus died, He cried out, *"It is finished!"* (Bible, Injil, John 19:30) What was finished? Jesus had finished taking the punishment that we deserve for our sin. He suffered, body and soul, in place of all those who trust in Him. But now His work was accomplished, finished. When Jesus died and went immediately to His Father's presence in paradise, He went in the company of that thief.

What wonderful good news this is! It means that all your sin can be forgiven. It means that you can be with Christ in paradise the moment you die.

But how can I get to heaven?

Can religion help?

Absolutely not! There are millions of people on this earth who have never seen the serious nature of sin. They have no idea that they will end up in hell for crimes that they consider trivial. They know that they have to face God after death, but they think that their religious works will buy their way out of any trouble in which they may find themselves. As long as they trivialize their sin, they deceive themselves into thinking that they can work their way into heaven by their religious works.

It is as futile as a man who was trying to row against a river. He was in a boat caught in fast-moving water, heading for a massive waterfall with jagged rocks 150 feet below. A passer-by saw him rowing against the current, but his efforts were futile. Minute by minute he was drawn closer and closer to the roaring falls. The passer-by ran to his car, grabbed a rope from the boot and threw it to the boat. When it fell across the bow, he shouted, "Grab the rope. I will pull you to the shore!" He couldn't believe his eyes, for the man in the boat took no notice. He just kept on rowing frantically against the current, until he disappeared over the edge of the falls to his death.

God is our only hope!

God Himself has thrown us a rope in Jesus Christ. He is the only One who can save us from death and hell. But we must let go of our own efforts to save ourselves and take hold of the rope. The moment we cease our own religious "rowing" and have faith in Jesus, we find peace with God. The Bible says, *"For by grace you have been saved through faith, and that not of yourselves; it is the gift of God, not of works, lest anyone should boast."* (Bible, Injil, Ephesians 2:8-9) It is unwise to reject God's saving plan. What do you think of the drowning man who refused to be saved?

Let me give you another illustration to show that religion can never save you. Imagine that one day you go swimming and jump into deep water. You find yourself in trouble. Drowning! You are dying, but you cannot save yourself because you do not know how to swim. You are hopeless and helpless. You shout for help. Someone approaches and yells, "Pull yourself together and save yourself! Come on mate, do it yourself!" What a terrible thing to say to a drowning man! A second person arrives on the scene and actually jumps into the water. He starts swimming. He says, "Look at me. Learn how to swim and do the same. Then you will save yourself". How ridiculous! There is no time for you to learn. In fact, a drowning man is absolutely incapable of learning anything. Now a third person approaches. He dives into the pool, grabs you and drags you out of the water. You might resist him, but out of compassion he saves you from death. Now, which one of these three people would you thank the most? Surely the third one.

Religion is like the first two people. By nature we are drowning in our sin. We are in a mess because of our separation from God. Religion tells us, like the first person who tries to help, "Save yourself. Do this and that. Don't do this or that and you will be saved." Some religious leaders, like the second person who jumps into the water, are presented as examples. Their followers are told that if they imitate their lifestyle, they will be saved.

Religion cannot save us. We are hopeless. The Bible says that we are incapable of saving ourselves. That is why we need someone to jump into the water of our life and get hold of us and save us from our sin.

That is exactly what God has done. He has provided a way for sinners to be brought back to Him. God says to us, "I know your situation. I know that you are separated from Me. I know that your life is in a mess. I know that you cannot save yourself. And I know that giving you laws and commandments will not save you because you can't and don't obey them. You are incapable of following them. But I will come to where you are and get you out of the tyranny of your sin."

So God came to this world in the Person of Jesus Christ. *"Christ also suffered once for sins, the just for the unjust, that He might bring us to God."* (Bible, 1 Peter 3:18) Jesus Christ took the punishment that we deserve for our sin. He bridged the insurmountable chasm that separates us from God.

So, how can I get to heaven?

Jesus is the way. He said, *"I am the way, the truth and the life. No one comes to the Father except through Me."* (Bible, Injil, John 14:6) Think about that thief on the cross next to Jesus. Was he promised paradise because of his good works? Did he have time to put his past life right? Well, he would be dead by 3 pm! He would have no time in six hours to put his life right even if he could get off the cross. Did he give to the poor? Did he fast? Don't get me wrong, these are good things to do, but THEY ARE NOT THE DOOR INTO PARADISE.

Do you have to be a special person to go to paradise? NO!

Do you have to be in a special place? NO!

Do you have to say special words? NO!

Do you have to have special accomplishments? NO!

So who goes to heaven? Everybody who clings to Christ, trusting in what He did for them on the cross. That is the only condition. When someone allows Jesus to save them (by trusting in His death and resurrection), Jesus forgives their sin and grants them a place in paradise. He will dismiss the case against them.

If people who trust in Jesus are sure of going to heaven, why don't they just live however they want?

Many people ask this question: 'If someone knows they are going to paradise, can they just do whatever they want, yet still be saved?'

We find the answer in the Bible: *"What shall we say then? Shall we continue in sin that grace may abound? Certainly not! How shall we who died to sin* [Christians] *live any longer in it?"* (Bible, Injil, Romans 6:1-2).

Jesus' death and resurrection were the focus of God's perfect plan to save sinners AND SET THEM FREE FROM SLAVERY TO SIN. The Bible says that the moment a person sincerely puts his trust in Jesus Christ and receives Him as Saviour and Lord, three great things happen:

1. He is saved (or set free) from the penalty of sin: God forgives all of that person's sin. God is just and fair. He must punish all the wrong things we do. But Jesus took the punishment that we deserve.

The price has been paid. "There is therefore now no condemnation to those who are in Christ Jesus." (Bible, Injil, Romans 8:1)

2. He is saved (or delivered) from the power of sin: God gives that person a new heart. Then He comes to live in it through His Holy Spirit. The person starts to look at life in a radically new way. He now hates sin and loves what is true and right. *"Therefore, if anyone is in Christ, he is a new creation; old things have passed away; behold, all things have become new."* (Bible, Injil, 2 Corinthians 5:17) The Bible also says, *"The fruit of the Spirit is love, joy, peace, longsuffering, kindness, goodness, faithfulness, gentleness, self-control."* (Bible, Injil, Galatians 5:22-23) These things will start to characterize that person's life because he has been made new and clean on the inside.

3. He shall be saved (or freed) from the presence of sin. One day Jesus Christ will come back to judge the world. On that day, He will punish those who rejected Him, but those who trusted in Him and followed His commands will be rewarded. He will deliver them from the presence of sin.

So anyone who says "I am forgiven and can do anything I like," cannot be a real Christian, since there is no evidence that the Holy Spirit is working in his life.

You can be sure of going to paradise

How terrible it is to live your live here on earth without knowing for sure whether or not you are going to heaven! I recently had the opportunity to talk with one market stallholder who sells Muslim books. I asked if he was sure that he was going to paradise. The man said, 'No one can be sure.' 'Then you may not go to paradise?' 'That's right.' 'So you may go to hell?' That made the man angry! 'How dare you tell me that I might go to hell!' Far be it from me to wish him to go to hell. With all respect to my Muslim friend, I found his reaction ironic. Well, to me it showed his frustration at the uncertainty of his future. It's a terrible thing!

The wonderful news is that God doesn't want to leave you in limbo. He wants you to be sure of going to paradise. Consider for instance what the Holy Scriptures say about the reason why God gave His Holy Word, the Bible: *"These are written that you may believe that Jesus is the Christ, the Son of God[2], and that believing you may have life in His name."* (Bible, Injil, John 20:31) *"These things I have written to you who believe in the name of the Son of God[3], that you may know that you have eternal life"* (Injil, 1 John 5:13). In these verses, God not only tells us that we can know for sure that we'll go to paradise, but also tells us how we can have that assurance.

Your eternal destiny is not decided by your good or bad works. Entrance into paradise is a free gift from God, received through faith in Jesus Christ. The Bible says, "For by grace you have been saved

---

[2] E.M. Hicham has written a booklet called, 'How can God have a Son?' Contact us if you'd like a free copy.

through faith, and that not of yourselves; it is the gift of God, not of works, lest anyone should boast." (Bible, Injil, Ephesians 2:8-9)

Will you be there?

My friend, God has given us a way to be saved from slavery to sin and from His judgment, a way to paradise. In paradise there is no sin, so there will be none of the sad and bad things that make life on earth so tough. This is what Jesus says to everyone who believes in Him: *"In My Father's house are many mansions; if it were not so, I would have told you. I go to prepare a place for you. And if I go and prepare a place for you, I will come again and receive you to Myself; that where I am, there you may be also."* (Bible, Injil, John 14:2-3) You can see why no Christian is afraid of the Day of Judgement! In fact, Christians look forward to Jesus' return. On that day He will send to hell all those who refused His free offer of salvation, but He will take His people home to paradise.

Jesus lived the blameless life that you and I should have lived, and He succeeded where you and I have failed. People mocked Him. They crucified Him. Yet all this fulfilled God's plan to rescue us from sin.

Will you confess your guilt to God and give your heart and life to Jesus Christ? Once you do that (like the thief on the cross), God promises to give you a new heart ... and to reserve a place for you in paradise!

E.M. Hicham

Quiz

If you have read this booklet carefully, you should be able to answer the following questions. These questions are arranged in the order of the chapters. I encourage you to re-read each corresponding chapter before you make your responses. We would love to see your answers. So why not send them to us at the following address:

Word of Hope Ministries
PO Box 24, Rochdale, OL16 3FB, UK

1. Have you ever thought about the two questions: Why weren't you born in heaven (paradise)? Why is there death?

2. What was God's original creation like?

3. On what condition did God say that man could stay in the Garden of Eden (جنة عدن)?

4. What did Adam and Eve do wrong?

5. What were the consequences?

6. Muslims believe that Adam and Eve sinned against God, but that they afterwards repented and that their repentance was accepted – with the effect that everything returned to normal. After reading this booklet, what would your reply be?

7. What does it mean for Adam to be a federal head?

8. Do people today experience the same consequences of sin as Adam and Eve did? In what way? And why?

9. What was God's remedy for man's sinful nature?

10. God's promise in Genesis 3:14-15 is about *the seed of the woman*. How did Jesus fulfill this promise?

11. So, why weren't we born in paradise?

12. What lesson(s) have you learnt from the story of the forgiven thief on the cross?

13. Can religion get you to heaven? Why?

14. How can you get to heaven (paradise)?

If you would like to receive further information,
please contact us.

If you wish to make further study of the
Christian faith correspondence courses
in English, Arabic and French are available from:

Word of Hope Ministries

Word of Hope Ministries
22 New St. Rochdale, OL16 3PQ

England

Email: **contact@word-of-hope.net**
Web: www.word-of-hope.net

Do you speak French?

www.Jesus-Islam.fr